SPIRITUALLY TRANSMITTED DEMONS

BEWARE

of

ANCIENT

STD's

BILLY E. CHATMAN JR.

Publisher's Name: Pastor Billy E. Chatman Jr.

ISBN: 978-1-962142-48-9

CONTENTS

Dedication 1

Foreword By 2

Acknowledgement.. 3

Introduction 5

Chapter 1: Who Is The God Called Molech In
The Old Testament? 13

Chapter 2: Who Is The Ancient God Called Baal?....... 19

Chapter 3: Who Was The Goddess Ashtoreth? 25

Chapter 4: "The Evil Trinity" 31

Chapter 5: The Spirt Leviathan.................................... 40

Chapter 6: "The Lord Of The Flies" 56

Chapter 7: "Night Terror Spirits".............................. 63

Chapter 8: Spirit Of Jezebel.. 75

Chapter 9: The Spirit Of Lilith.................................... 83

Chapter 10: The Place Of Power And Authority 87

About The Author 96

Conclusion.. 98

DEDICATION

This book is dedicated to my beautiful wife, Nicci, of 31 years, who has always been my biggest supporter. You are the love of my life. To my son, Billy III, and my daughter, Reonna, who is my pride and joy. To my mother and father, Sharon & and Billy Chatman Sr., who have always had my back all the way from childhood. To my brother, Curtis, who is having his first baby boy at 54 years of age. To my Aunt Barbara, who has always supported my ministry from the time I started pastoring. To my church family, Tampa Revival Center, thank you for all your support. We have come a long way, but the best is yet to come.

This book is also dedicated to the body of Christ as a whole. To the mighty men and women of God who have gone before us and paved the way for future generations to come. To the prayer warriors and mothers of the church who have prayed many of us out of the pits of hell, I personally want to thank you. My mother is one of those old prayer warriors that many churches are missing today. If it weren't for her praying, I don't know where I would be.

FOREWORD BY

Bishop George Dawson

As you well know by now, this world is filled with Diseases. We've recently, in the past few years experienced COVID, and who knows what is next to hit this planet. There is a whole church world called the Kingdom of God, the church, or the body of Christ. After examining the new book by Pastor Billy Chatman, I've come to the conclusion that we're suffering from STD Syndrome. Chatman has gracefully researched and testified beautifully about himself and his deliverance. This is a must-read!! Here's my conclusion after examining this thread of information from the book: You can be saved but not delivered. We're shouting, but we're sick. Speaking in tongues, but sick. Laying hands, but still sick. Is there a balm in Gilead? Is there healing for this nation? Pastor Billy E. Chatman Jr. gives us the answer.

ACKNOWLEDGEMENT

First and foremost, I give all glory and honor to God, whose guidance and wisdom have been my constant source of strength throughout the creation of this book, "Beware of Ancient STD's."

I am deeply grateful to my family, whose unwavering support and encouragement have been invaluable. To my loving wife, Nikita L Chatman, thank you for your patience, understanding, and belief in my vision. To my children, Billy III & Reonna, your love and joy have been my inspiration.

A heartfelt thank you to my editor, Skylark Media, whose keen eye and insightful feedback have greatly enhanced the clarity and impact of this work. Your dedication and expertise have been instrumental in bringing this book to life.

I would also like to express my gratitude to my church family at Tampa Revival Center, whose prayers and support have been a blessing. Your faith in my ministry and this message has been a driving force in my journey.

Special thanks to my mentor, Bishop George Dawson & Bishop Aubrey Shines, for your guidance and wisdom. Your teachings have profoundly influenced my understanding and have been a cornerstone in the development of this book.

Lastly, to all the readers and supporters of this work, thank you for embarking on this journey with me. It is my hope that this book will enlighten and inspire you as much as the process of writing it has for me.

With sincere appreciation,

Pastor Billy E. Chatman Jr

INTRODUCTION

The Bible is filled with countless stories of supernatural beings, including demons, that have fascinated and terrified readers for centuries. These beings are often described as malevolent entities that seek to harm and deceive humans, tempting them away from righteousness and into sin. In the ancient world, demons were believed to be the cause of various afflictions, from physical illnesses to mental disorders, and were often invoked in magical rites and exorcisms. This book delves into the fascinating world of ancient demons from the Bible, exploring their origins, characteristics, and roles in biblical stories. Through a combination of historical research and literary analysis, readers will gain a deeper understanding of these mysterious beings and the ways in which they have shaped our understanding of the supernatural.

This book is about learning how to keep the enemy from gaining access to your soul. The soul is like a black box. It goes back to the maker when your time on earth is done. It records all your activities on earth. The body which we feed, clothe and pamper will eventually decay and turn to dust.

If ever there was a time when our homes and families were under attack by the powers of Satan, it is in the day and time in which we live.

I don't believe in looking for a demon under every rock, and I don't think that we should be unbalanced when we talk about spiritual warfare. But the truth is, as Apostle Paul said, "We wrestle not against flesh and blood, but against principalities and powers, and spiritual rulers of darkness in this world." (Ephesians 6:12)

When I was 13, we lived in the Philippines because my father was in the Air Force, stationed at Clark Air Base. One evening, I spent the night with a friend who happened to be our next-door neighbor. He took me to a place where children had no business being because he wanted to celebrate my birthday. Three days later, I contracted an STD, all because I was doing things that I had no business doing. It was the worst thing that a thirteen-year-old could ever experience. I will never forget this experience as long as I live. Three days after having sex with a total stranger, I began to feel a burning sensation when going to the restroom. Now I had to figure out how I was going to tell my parents that I was having this burning sensation. Years later, I discovered after being called into ministry that contracting an STD is like what happens when people open themselves up to demonic activity. But instead of it being a physical encounter, it is a spiritual one.

I understand what the Bible was saying when it said we must guard our eye gates and ear gates because those are the gateways to your soul. Many believers as well as unbelievers have opened themselves up to demonic activity and have allowed Satan and the forces of darkness to penetrate their souls. Why are so many believers sleeping with the enemy? This book will identify the ancient spirits of this world that continue to attack the believers of the 21st century. This book will also teach you how to close demonic portals that you had no idea were open in your life. Go with me on a journey of spiritual warfare and defeating the demonic forces that have been attacking you and your families since days of old.

Do you know that the devil isn't after you but after your soul? It's your responsibility to feed and guard your soul. Feed your soul by reading and practicing the word of God. Guard your soul by protecting channels leading to it. These channels are what I call "spiritual gates."

Times are crucial, the devil is working tirelessly to possess the souls of careless Christians, who would serve as his guests in the lake of fire.

WHAT ARE SPIRITUAL GATES?

Spiritual gates are the channels or the doorways to one's soul. For example, blood is a channel to the heart. If the blood is contaminated, the heart suffers. However, the spiritual gateway to the soul includes body portals like the eyes, ears, mouth, and so on. These gates are the areas the devil uses to gain access to manipulate your soul, steal your God-given gifts and vision, and use you to fulfill demonic operations and destruction. The devil comes to steal, kill, and destroy. John 10: 10a

SPIRITUAL GATES EXPLAINED AND HOW TO OVERCOME THE DEVIL

In **Ephesians 6:12**, the Bible makes us understand that our struggle is not against flesh and blood, but against the rulers, the authorities, and the powers of this dark world and against the spiritual forces of evil in the heavenly realms. **This** means evil exists in the world today and we must defend our souls through spiritual warfare by God's grace. We do that by guarding the spiritual gates to the soul. These are some of the measures the devil uses to manipulate the soul.

GUARD YOUR EYES

"The eyes are windows to the soul." The eyes are gateways through which information enters the mind. What are you feeding your eyes? The devil has projected ways to manipulate our souls through the eyes, hence the lust of the eye. The Bible describes the eye as the lamp of the body. If your eyes are healthy, your whole body will be full of light. But if your eyes are unhealthy, your whole body will be full of darkness. Matt 6:22.

The sin of sexual immorality always starts from the eyes. To demonstrate, David committed sexual sin with Bathsheba after he saw her naked body. 2 Samuel 11: 2-5. Matthew 5:28 says that everyone who looks at a woman with lustful intent has already committed adultery with her in his heart.

So, therefore, to avoid lust of the eyes, greed, and more, use your eyes to read the word of God. Be mindful of what you watch on TV, social media, etc. Learn to move your neck or close your eyes when you see forbidden things. Pray to God and ask Him for help. In fact, discipline your eyes to limit the devil from manipulating your soul. Be like Job who made a covenant with God not to look lustfully at anything immoral. Job 31:1

GUARD YOUR EARS

In the same way, the ear is another major gateway to the soul. What you hear can impact you in a positive or negative way. The devil deceived Eve by convincing her to eat the forbidden fruit. The ears of Christians should be tuned to gaining wisdom and understanding so that we will fear the Lord and gain His knowledge **Proverbs**

2:2 &5. The devil is very crafty; he makes use of music, movies, and the media to defile our ears. Secure your ear gates; avoid gossip, idle jokes, worldly music, curse words, and so on. Use your ears to seek the word of God. Surround yourself with positive people who speak encouraging words and desire the same goal of heaven at last.

Jesus is coming soon and only those who have received Him will make it to heaven. Be on the lookout so the devil doesn't use your body as an instrument to manipulate your soul and the people around you. When the devil gets your soul, he steals your purpose and dominates your body for the purpose of destruction. Therefore, put on the whole armor of God and ~~to~~ be strong in the Lord.

GUARD OUR MOUTH

Your mouth is also a gateway in your life. Although it is a one-way street with traffic flowing out instead of in, your words will not only affect your life, but they are powerful in their working. The Bible says that *Job did not sin with his lips.* (Job 2:10) and that *life and death are in the power of the tongue* (Proverbs 18:21). What is brewing in your heart because of what's been allowed through the gateways of your eyes and ears often is shared from your mouth with others.

The Bible is clear that our homes ought to be places where God is honored. Are we speaking life or death to our spouses and our children? Do our conversations serve to uplift them or cause them to feel discouraged and ashamed? Jesus said, "The good person out of the good treasure of his heart produces good, and the evil person out of his evil treasure produces evil, for out of the abundance of the heart his mouth speaks" (Luke 6:45). Again, "life & and death are in the power of the tongue!" So, what can we do to guard our gates?

Scripture shows us repeatedly that our defense is in the blood of the Lamb. Hebrews 12:24 tells us the blood of Christ "speaks a better word than the blood of Abel." When we take communion in our homes, when we take the bread, which symbolizes His body, and the fruit of the vine, which symbolizes His blood, then we allow God's peace, joy, righteousness, and redemptive work to have its way in our hearts and homes.

With the help of the Holy Spirit, we can guard our eyes, mouths, and ears by filling them with the word of God. Philippians 4:6-8 tells us, "Do not be anxious about anything, but in every situation, by prayer and petition, with thanksgiving, present your requests to God. And the peace of God, which transcends all understanding, will guard your hearts and your minds in Christ Jesus. Finally, brothers and sisters, whatever is true, whatever is noble, whatever is right, whatever is pure, whatever is lovely, whatever is admirable—if anything is excellent or praiseworthy—think about such things."

CHAPTER 1

WHO IS THE GOD CALLED MOLECH IN THE OLD TESTAMENT?

Molech was an ancient Canaanite god associated with child sacrifice. The Hebrew word "Molech" appears only once in the Bible, in Leviticus 18:21, where it is forbidden as an abomination. There is some debate over the exact identity of Molech. He is most likely a deity who was worshiped by the Ammonites and Moabites. The practice of child sacrifice was common in many cultures throughout history. It was particularly abhorrent to the Israelites.

Children are innocent and helpless and therefore represent the purest form of devotion. Offering them up to an evil god is a betrayal of their trust and innocence. The prophets condemned those who offered their children to Molech as being guilty of the most heinous crime. In Jeremiah 32:35, God said this: *They built the high places of Baal in the Valley of Ben Hinnom to burn their sons and daughters in the fire as offerings to Baal.* In conclusion, the prophet Isaiah described Molech as a "grim god who delighted in human suffering." (Isaiah 57:15).

The Bible does not give a clear answer as to why child sacrifice was considered so heinous. However, it may be because Molech was one of the most feared gods in the ancient Near East. His worship involved some of the most gruesome rituals imaginable. Victims were often burned alive in giant metal statues of the god. This was an act that was supposed to bring favor from Molech and ensure a bountiful harvest. The horrific practice of child sacrifice was finally outlawed by the Israelites under King Josiah in the seventh century BC.

There is evidence that child sacrifice continued to be practiced in some parts of the Near East. This went on until well into the first century AD. The abhorrent practice of child sacrifice was eventually stamped out throughout the world. However, it still occurs in some cultures today. Sadly, the memory of Molech lives on as a symbol of barbarity and evil.

For the past 50 years, the spirit of Molech has plagued our nation. Ever since abortion was ruled legal after the Roe vs. Wade case in 1973. American women aborted 1.2 million babies per year before abortion was made illegal. If you calculate that by 50 years, it comes out to be over 60 million babies over that time period. America has a lot of blood on its hands. These aborted babies are crying out from the ground. It is disturbing when you think about the consequences that are coming to our nation because of killing the innocent. America will not be able to escape the judgment of our God.

Many women have been hunted by the spirit of Molech. Many are tormented by a guilty conscience for what they have done to their unborn babies. Satan would love for you to take that guilty conscience to your grave, but the Bible says, "There is therefore no condemnation to those that are in Christ Jesus." Romans 8:1-3. Don't allow the enemy to hold you hostage for something that God has already forgiven!

My prayer for you if you're still struggling with the guilt of abortion:

Heavenly Father, we lift up all the women and mothers who freely and willingly chose to abort their babies, thinking that a baby in their life would spoil the plans they had made or inhibit their desired future. We pray for Your mercy and forgiveness over each one and ask that in a very special way, you would come alongside each woman who terminated her pregnancy. Meet each one at her very point of need and lead her to repentance. Will you please comfort those who are grieving, support those who are weak, and convict those who have rejected the sacredness of a human life? Bring each one to a saving faith in the Lord Jesus, and an assurance of Your gracious forgiveness. This we ask in Jesus' name, Amen.

Lord, "comfort the fainthearted, uphold the weak." (1 Thessalonians 5:14).

Say this prayer for healing if you have had an abortion:

Oh Lord, I had an abortion thinking it was for the best, but the grief and guilt I have felt ever since I made that decision has haunted me, and I feel so ashamed of myself and riddled with guilt, for allowing a little life to be taken in this way. I realize more and more that it is against You Lord, that I have sinned and done this great wrong. Lord, I feel broken inside and pray for Your forgiveness, healing, and comfort. Thank You that You are a forgiving God, whose mercies are new every morning, and that You have promised to carry all our guilt and burdens. I hand this over to You today and ask for the healing and restoration that only You can give, and the grace to forget what is past and move on with You as my guide. I ask this in the name of Jesus, Amen.

"A broken and a contrite heart, oh Lord, You will never despise." (Psalm 51:17).

My prayer for the healing of fathers mourning an abortion:

Loving Heavenly Father, we pray for the fathers of aborted babies and the emotional trauma that affects them, knowing that they are sometimes excluded from the decision to terminate a pregnancy. We pray that You would be close to those who have been left emotionally distraught and grieving for the little life that they were denied. We pray for Your comfort upon all men who have been affected by abortion in this way as they grieve for the son or daughter that they will never know. We ask this in Jesus' name, Amen.

Father, strengthen the hearts of all those who hope in You. **Be strong and take heart, all you who hope in the Lord. Be of good courage, and he shall strengthen your heart, All ye that hope in the Lord.** (Psalm 31:24)

My prayer for mothers considering an abortion:

Heavenly Father, we lift up the many mothers who are today considering an abortion and pray that in Your grace You would direct them to make a Godly and wise decision. Lord, you know their individual circumstances and the many conflicts flooding their minds of whether or not to abort the baby in their womb. Send them Godly counselors, wise advisors, and caring friends to come alongside them, to offer them guidance, hope, and comfort. Reassure them that abortion is not the answer to what seems to be a problem and help them to recognize that You are the Author of life and hope. Instill in the heart of each pregnant woman a deep love for the baby she is carrying. We pray that many may be prompted to turn from their planned abortion and look to the Lord Jesus, for the grace to do what is right. In the name of Jesus, Amen.

Reveal Yourself to these mothers, o Lord, as their hiding place and shield; let them find hope in Your Word. (Psalm 119:114).

CHAPTER 2

WHO IS THE ANCIENT GOD CALLED BAAL?

Baal was the name of the supreme god worshiped in ancient Canaan and Phoenicia. The practice of Baal worship infiltrated Jewish religious life during the time of the Judges (Judges 3:7), became widespread in Israel during the reign of Ahab (1 Kings 16:31-33), and also affected Judah (2 Chronicles 28:1-2). The word *Baal* means *lord*; the plural is *Baalism*. In general, Baal was a fertility god who was believed to enable the earth to produce crops and people to produce children. Different regions worshiped Baal in different ways, and Baal proved to be a highly adaptable god. Various locales emphasized one or another of his attributes and developed special "denominations" of Baalism. Baal of Peor (Numbers 25:3) and Baal-Berith (Judges 8:33) are two examples of such localized deities.

According to Canaanite mythology, Baal was the son of El, the chief god, and Asherah, the goddess of the sea. Baal was considered the most powerful of all gods, eclipsing El, who was seen as rather weak and ineffective. In various battles, Baal defeated Yamm, the god of the sea, and Mot, the god of death and the underworld. Baal's sisters/consorts were Ashtoreth, a fertility goddess associated with the stars, and Anath, a goddess of love and war. The Canaanites worshiped Baal as the sun god and as the storm god—he is usually depicted holding a lightning bolt—who defeated enemies and produced crops. They also worshiped him as a fertility god who provided children. Baal worship was rooted in sensuality and involved ritualistic prostitution in the temples. At times, appeasing Baal required human sacrifice, usually the firstborn of the one making the sacrifice (Jeremiah 19:5). The priests of Baal appealed to their god in rites of wild abandon which included loud, ecstatic cries and self-inflicted injury (1 Kings 18:28).

Before the Hebrews entered the Promised Land, the Lord God warned against worshiping Canaan's gods (Deuteronomy 6:14-15), but Israel turned to idolatry anyway. During the reign of Ahab and Jezebel, at the height of Baal worship in Israel, God directly confronted paganism through His prophet Elijah. First, God showed that He, not Baal, controlled the rain by sending a drought lasting three-and-one-half years (1 Kings 17:1). Then Elijah called for a showdown on Mt. Carmel to prove once and for all who the true God was. All day long, 450 prophets of Baal called on their god to send fire from heaven—surely an easy task for a god associated with lightning bolts—but "there was no response, no one answered, no one paid attention" (1 Kings 18:29). After Baal's prophets gave up, Elijah prayed a simple prayer, and God answered immediately with fire from heaven. The evidence was overwhelming, and the people "feel prostrate and cried, 'The LORD! He is God! The LORD! He is God!'" (Verse 39).

Throughout the Old Testament in the Bible, we find what seems a confusing trend of idol worship among the Israelites, who especially struggled with the worship of Baal and Asherah (or Ashtoreth). God had commanded Israel not to worship idols (Exodus 20:3; Deuteronomy 5:7)—indeed, they were to avoid even mentioning a false god's name (Exodus 23:13). They were warned not to intermarry with the pagan nations and to avoid practices that might be construed as pagan worship rites (Leviticus 20:23; 2 Kings 17:15; Ezekiel 11:12). Israel was a nation chosen by God to one day bear the Savior of the world, Jesus Christ. Yet, even with so much riding on their heritage and future, Israel continued to struggle with idol worship.

After the death of Joshua, the worship of Baal and Asherah became a plague upon the Israelites and was a perennial problem. Baal, also known as the sun god or the storm god, is the name of the supreme male deity worshiped by ancient Phoenicians and Canaanites. Asherah, the moon goddess, was the principal female deity worshiped by ancient Syrians, Phoenicians, and Canaanites. The Israelites neglected to heed the Lord's warning not to compromise with idolaters. The ensuing generations forgot the God who had rescued them from Egypt (Judges 2:10–12).

Of course, the period of the judges wasn't the first time Israel had been tempted by idol worship. In Exodus 32, we see how quickly the Israelites gave up on Moses' return from Mount Sinai and created an idol of gold for themselves. Ezekiel 20 reveals a summary of the Israelites' affairs with idols and God's relentless mercy on His children (also see 1 & 2 Samuel, 1 & 2 Kings, 1 & 2 Chronicles).

As for why the worship of Baal and Asherah *specifically* was such a problem for Israel, there are several reasons we can cite: first, the worship of Baal and Asherah held the allure of illicit sex since the religion involved ritual prostitution. This is exactly what we see in the incident of Baal of Peor, as "the men began to indulge in sexual immorality with Moabite women, who invited them to the sacrifices to their gods" (Numbers 25:1–2). It was during this episode that an Israelite named Zimri brazenly brought a Midianite woman into the camp and went straight to his tent, where the two began having sex (verses 6–8, 14).

Another reason that the worship of Baal and Asherah was a perennial problem for Israel is due to what we could call national peer pressure. Israel wanted to be like the other nations (see 1 Samuel 8:5, 20). The other nations worshiped Baal and Asherah, and so many Israelites felt a pull to do the same.

Of course, we cannot overlook the fact of Satan's temptations and mankind's basic sinfulness. The enemy of our souls tempted Israel to worship idols; the sacrifices made to Baal and Asherah were really sacrifices to demons (1 Corinthians 10:20). The stubborn willfulness of humanity works in tandem with Satan's seductions and causes us to jump at any chance to rebel against God. Thus, Israel repeatedly forsook God's commands, despite losing God's blessings, and chased after the Baals and Asherahs to their own destruction.

The book of Hosea aptly uses adultery as a metaphor in describing Israel's problem with idol worship. The Israelites were trapped in a vicious cycle of idol worship, punishment, restoration, and then forgiveness, after which they went back to their idols once more. God's patience with Israel is unfathomable by human standards; God's nature is the essence of love, and He gives His sons and daughters chances to repent (1 John 4:8; Romans 8:38–39; 2 Peter 3:9).

The problem of Baal and Asherah worship was finally solved after God removed Israel from the Promised Land. Due to the Israelites' idolatry and disregard of the Law, God brought the nations of Assyria and Babylon against them in an act of judgment. After the exile, Israel was restored to the land, and the people did not dally again with idols.

While Christians today may be quick to judge the Israelites for their idolatry, we must remember that idols take many forms. Idolatrous sins still lure and tempt the modern-day believer (Romans 3:23; 1 John 1:8–10), though perhaps they have taken new manifestations. Instead of ancient forms of Baal and Asherah, we today sometimes honor possessions, success, physical pleasure, and religious perfection to the dishonor of God. Just as God disciplined the Israelites for their idolatry and forgave them when they repented, He will graciously discipline us and extend the offer of forgiveness in Christ (Hebrews 12:7–11; 1 John 1:9; 2 Peter 3:9).

CHAPTER 3

WHO WAS THE GODDESS ASHTORETH?

Ashtoreth is one of the main false gods mentioned in the Old Testament. Different groups have different thoughts on who Ashtoreth was and what she was associated with. Still, most modern consensus agrees that Ashtoreth's name in scripture is a corruption of the name Astarte and that she was one of the chief female deities found in the region of Canaan.

WHERE DOES THE BIBLE MENTION ASHTORETH?

A false goddess in the Old Testament, Ashtoreth was one of the many gods Israel turned to instead of YAHWEH. Ashtoreth is mentioned several times throughout Judges, 1 and 2 Samuel, and 1 and 2 Kings. Her worship was a direct violation of the first of the Ten Commandments God gave to the Israelites after he saved them from Egypt:

You shall have no other gods before me. You shall not make for yourself an image in the form of anything in heaven above or on the earth beneath or in the waters below. You shall not bow down to them or worship them; for I, the Lord your God, am a jealous God, punishing the children for the sin of the parents to the third and fourth generation of those who hate me, but showing love to a thousand generations of those who love me and keep my commandments. (**Exodus 20:3-6**)

Though these verses do not mention Ashtoreth in particular, they provide an important context for Israelite interactions with Ashtoreth and other false gods.

Judges is the first place where Ashtoreth's name is specifically mentioned, telling us little except that she was a popular false goddess. Judges mention Ashtoreth's name twice in two nearly identical verses (**Judges 2:13**; **Judges 3:7**). In both verses, Israel has turned away from worshiping God and instead began worshiping Baal and Ashtoreth. In these verses, Ashtoreth's name refers to any and all female deities Israel worshiped. From this, we can surmise that the worship of Ashtoreth herself was so common that she had become synonymous with all false god worship, similar to how the modern consumer refers to all bandages by the well-known brand name Band-Aid. The book of 1 Samuel also used Ashtoreth's name in this manner.

We learn more about Ashtoreth in 1 and 2 Kings. In **1 King 11**, King Solomon opens a temple for her in Jerusalem to appease one of his many foreign wives. Here is where we first learn that Ashtoreth was specifically related to the Phoenician city of Sidon.

Ashtoreth worship, along with that of the goddess Asherah, was spread even more during the reign of King Ahab. His wife Jezebel was a Phoenician princess. As queen, Jezebel brought in dozens of false priests with her to Israel. The prophet Elijah faces off with these priests.

Many modern Hebrew scholars believe that Ashtoreth's name shows God's contempt for Israel's dalliances with false gods, as the Bible is the only place that refers to this goddess Ashtoreth. Ashtoreth's name seems to combine the goddess's real name Astarte with the Hebrew word for shame, boshet.

Ashtoreth may be mentioned in other areas throughout scripture. However, it can be difficult to figure out what verses specifically refer to her for two reasons. Firstly, it can be difficult to differentiate Ashtoreth from the goddess Asherah (especially since many believe both goddesses were worshiped in tree groves known as Asherah). Secondly, many verses do not mention

Ashtoreth by name. Many biblical scholars have connected Ashtoreth with the worship of the moon mentioned in **2 Kings 23:5** and with the Queen of Heaven mentioned in **Jeremiah 7:18**.

WHAT COUNTRY WORSHIPED ASHTORETH?

As mentioned above, Ashtoreth is connected to Phoenicia, especially its city of Sidon. However, her reach throughout the ancient world went much further than the borders of Phoenicia. Many of Phoenicia's most populous cities were famous seaports. Along with trading goods throughout the ancient world, Phoenicia also spread its culture.

As such, Ashtoreth's cult spread throughout Canaan, Egypt, and Ugarit. In 1 Samuel, we see that the Philistines also worshipped her. Over time, her cult evolved, and her worship often intermingled with that of other deities. Parts of Ashtoreth's cult influenced the worship of the Mesopotamian goddess Ishtar; the Egyptian goddesses Isis and Hathor; and the Greco-Roman deities of Aphrodite, Juno, and Artemis.

In the form of the Ephesian Artemis, Ashtoreth continued to impact scripture in the New Testament. In **Acts 19**, Paul faced off against her believers and barely escaped with his life.

WHAT DID ASHTORETH WORSHIPPERS DO?

Ashtoreth was worshipped as the goddess of a wide variety of things. She was connected with both the moon and the planet Venus. **Easton's Bible Dictionary** says she represented "the passive principle in nature." She was also seen as a goddess of fertility, sexual love, and war.

Her worshippers raised Asherah poles in her name. They also engaged in what **Smith's Bible Dictionary** refers to as "the most impure rites." This may have included sacrifices, cutting, and sexual acts. **Jeremiah 44** says that Canaanites burned offerings and poured out libations to her.

WHY SHOULD WE KNOW ABOUT ASHTORETH TODAY?

It isn't difficult to understand why the Israelites continuously turned away from the one true God to false gods like Ashtoreth. The one true God never promises a perfect life, but we humans long for one. We also long to be free to act as we wish. Even though God showed the Israelites many wonders, He also created an intricate law code for them to follow. In contrast, those around the Israelites got to live as they pleased, worshipping gods who promised fertility and protection if they worshipped them in just the right way. Even though the worship of Ashtoreth included acts that would make many of us blush, there was an allure to her promises and popularity.

Though Christians today may not run after literal gods, we often chase things with that same worshipful ferocity. We see others chasing these things, and we think, "God doesn't promise an easy life, but wealth/fame/pleasure/love/etcetera might!" We make things our gods and ignore the ones we are meant to follow wholeheartedly. Matthew 6:24 tells us that we can't serve God to our fullest if we worship something else, just as the Israelites could not, please God while following Ashtoreth. Whenever you read of Israel's idolatry, consider where idolatry is in your own life.

CHAPTER 4

"THE EVIL TRINITY"

Satan has his own trinity—the devil, the beast, and the false prophet (Revelation 16:13). He has his own church, "a synagogue of Satan" (Revelation 2:9). He has his own ministers, "ministers of Satan" (2 Corinthians 11:4-5). He has formulated his own system of theology: "doctrines of demons" (1 Timothy 4:1). He has established his own sacrificial system: "The Gentiles...sacrifice to demons" (1 Corinthians 10:20). He has his own communion service: "the cup of demons...and the table of demons" (1 Corinthians 10:21).

His ministers proclaim his own gospel: "a gospel contrary to that which we have preached to you" (Galatians 1:7-8). He has his own throne (Revelation 13:2) and his own worshipers (Revelation 13:4). So, he has developed a thorough imitation of Christianity, viewed as a system of religion. In his role as the imitator of God, he inspires false Christs, self-constituted messiahs (Matthew 24:4-5). He employs false teachers who are specialists in his "theology" to bring in "destructive heresies, even denying the Master who bought them" (2 Peter 2:1).

They are adept at mixing truth and error in such proportions as to make error palatable. They carry on their teaching surreptitiously and often anonymously. He sends out false prophets: "And many false prophets will arise and will mislead many" (Matthew 24:11). He introduces false brethren into the church, who "had sneaked in to spy out our liberty...in order to bring us into bondage" (Galatians 2:4). He sponsors false apostles who imitate the true (2 Corinthians 11:13).

The Trinity of Evil was once three angels, Belial, Mephistopheles, and Asmodeus, who rebelled against God 10 billion years ago (This was referred to as the second civil war in Heaven, the first presumably being that led by Lucifer) because they did not believe that they should bow to mortals.

The Trinity was then sealed in the Netherworld, where they devoted their lives to discovering forbidden knowledge. They built large structures in the netherworld and eventually came to lead the countless Wraiths of the netherworld, as well as their queen, Zaphora. They were also involved, somehow, with the imprisonment of Apollyon. Eventually seeking to conquer Hell, the Trinity hired Pagan to rid Lady Hell of Lady Death, and they sent their legions to help conquer Hell.

A common tactic of Satan is to imitate or counterfeit the things of God in order to make himself appear to be like God. What is commonly referred to as the "unholy trinity," described vividly in Revelations 12 and 13, is no exception. The three-in-one God consists of God the Father, the Son Jesus Christ, & the Holy Spirit. All three are one. Their counterparts in the unholy trinity are Satan, the Antichrist, and the False Prophet. While the true and living God is characterized by infinite truth, love, and goodness, the unholy three portray dramatically opposite traits of deception, hatred, and unadulterated evil.

Revelation 12 and 13 contain prophetic passages that describe some of the main events and the figures involved during the second half of the seven-year Tribulation period. Although many Bible passages allude to Satan in various forms, such as a serpent or an angel of light, he is described in Revelation 12:3 as a "great red dragon, having seven heads and ten horns, and seven crowns upon his heads." The color red indicates his vicious and homicidal personality. The seven heads symbolize seven evil kingdoms that Satan has empowered and used throughout history to attempt to prevent God's ultimate plan from coming to fruition. Five of the kingdoms have already come and gone— Egypt, Assyria, Babylon, Medo-Persia, and Greece.

All these kingdoms severely oppressed and persecuted the Hebrews, killing many of them. Satan's intent was to prevent the birth of Christ (Revelation 12:4). The sixth kingdom, Rome, was still in existence during the writing of this prophecy. Under Roman rule, King Herod murdered Hebrew babies around the time of Christ's birth and Pontius Pilate ultimately authorized the crucifixion of Jesus. The seventh kingdom, which is fiercer and crueler than the others, will be the final world kingdom that the Antichrist forms during the end times. These kingdoms were also prophesied in Daniel, chapters 2 and 7. The seven crowns represent universal rule, and the ten horns represent complete world power or authority.

Revelation 12 indicates many important facts about Satan. Satan and one-third of the angels were cast out of heaven during a rebellion before the world began (Revelation 12:4). The Archangel Michael and the other angels will make war with Satan and his demons, and Satan will be excluded from heaven forever (Revelation 12:7-9). In his attempt to prevent God's fulfillment of His earthly kingdom, Satan will attempt to annihilate the Jews, but God will supernaturally protect a remnant of the Jews in a location outside of Israel for the last 42 months of the Tribulation (Revelation 12:6, 13–17; Matthew 24:15–21).

The second member of the unholy trinity is the Beast or Antichrist described in Revelation 13 and Daniel 7. The beast comes out of the sea, which typically in the Bible refers to the Gentile nations. He also has seven heads and ten horns, indicating his connection to and indwelling by Satan. The ten horns indicate ten seats of world government that will provide power to the Antichrist, three of which will be totally yielded to or taken over by the Antichrist (Daniel 7:8). The number ten also indicates completion or totality; in other words, a one-world government. The one-world government will be blasphemous, denying the true God. The final kingdom will possess traits in common with the former "beast kingdoms" of Babylon, Medo-Persia, Greece, and particularly Rome (Revelation 13:2; Daniel 7:7, 23). Revelation 13:3 seems to indicate that the Antichrist will be mortally wounded about halfway through the Tribulation, but Satan will miraculously heal his wound (Revelation 13:3; 17:8–14). After this wondrous event, the world will be totally enthralled by the Antichrist. They will worship Satan and the Antichrist himself (Revelation 13:4–5). The Antichrist becomes emboldened and, dispensing with all pretenses of being a peaceful ruler, he openly blasphemes God, breaks his peace treaty with the Jews, attacks believers and the Jews, and desecrates the rebuilt Jewish temple, setting himself up as the one to be worshiped (Revelation 13:4–

7; Matthew 24:15). This particular event has been called the Abomination of Desolation.

The final personage of the unholy trinity is the False Prophet, described in Revelation 13:11–18. This second beast comes out of the earth, not the sea, possibly indicating that he will be an apostate Jew coming from Israel. Although he presents himself as a meek, mild, and benevolent person, the horns indicate that he will have power. Jesus expressly warned believers to watch out for false prophets that may look innocent but can be very destructive (Matthew 7:15). The False Prophet speaks like a dragon, meaning that he will speak persuasively and deceptively to turn humans away from God and promote the worship of the Antichrist and Satan (Revelation 13:11–12). The False Prophet is capable of producing great signs and wonders, including bringing down fire from heaven (Revelation 13:13). He sets up an image of the Antichrist for worship, gives life to the image, demands the worship of the image from all people, and executes those who refuse to worship the image (Revelation 13:14–15). Revelation 20:4 indicates that the method of execution will be beheading.

The False Prophet will also compel each person to receive a permanent mark of some kind, just as slaves did in John's day, to show total devotion to the Antichrist and renunciation of God. Only those who receive the mark will be permitted to engage in commerce. Acceptance of the mark means eternal death (Revelation 14:10). The Bible makes clear that humans will fully understand that, by accepting the mark, they are not only accepting an economic system but also a worship system that rejects Jesus Christ. Revelation 13:18 reveals the number of the Beast—666. No one knows precisely what this means. Some believe that the Antichrist's first, middle, and last names will have six letters each. Some believe that the designation refers to a computer chip since some computer programs start with 666.

Satan is the anti-God, the Beast is the anti-Christ, and the False Prophet is the anti-Spirit. This unholy trinity will persecute believers and deceive many others, resulting in their eternal death. But God's kingdom will prevail. Daniel 7:21–22 states, "I was watching, and the same horn was making war against the saints and prevailing against them until the Ancient of Days came, and a judgment was made in favor of the saints of the Most High, and the time came for the saints to possess the kingdom."

The Bible very clearly predicts that as the world moves through the end-time judgments, men and women here on the earth will be controlled by three persons. Revelation 12 talks about the activity of Satan during the last days. Revelation 13 talks about a great political leader (the Antichrist) and a great religious leader (the

False Prophet). These three persons form an unholy trinity. Satan stands in contrast to God. The Man of Sin stands in contrast to Jesus Christ. The False Prophet stands in contrast to the Holy Spirit. During the Tribulation Period, the world will be governed and controlled by this unholy trinity of beings.

The latter half of Revelation 14 assures the reader of the ultimate triumph of Jesus Christ and of the final judgment of the wicked. In verse 8, an angel announces the fall of Babylon. In verses 9-11, another angel talks about the eternal torment of those who worship the Antichrist. In verse 13, still another voice talks about the blessedness of those who die in Christ. Verse 10 describes the doom of those who deny the Lord. "The same shall drink of the wine of the wrath of God." Verse 13 describes the eternal rest for those who are faithful to Him. "And I heard a voice from heaven saying unto me, Write, blessed are the dead which die in the Lord." Verse 11 makes it clear that there is no second chance after death. Those who worship the beast will suffer forever and ever.

And then finally in Rev. 14:15, another angel will announce that the harvest is ripe, and the hour of judgment has come. Read Revelation 14:15-16; 14:19-20. It is altogether possible that there are people living today who will hear the angel make the announcement described in these verses. You can angrily cast off all thoughts about such coming doom, and you can declare that a God of love would never pour out such judgments upon mankind—but the Bible repeatedly says that severe judgments are coming. Just as grapes are crushed in the winepress, so the enemies of God (at Armageddon) will be crushed under the wrath of God. And when the winepress of humanity is trodden down, Revelation 14:20 says the blood will become a river throughout an entire valley.

CHAPTER 5

THE SPIRT LEVIATHAN

The "leviathan spirit," or the "spirit of leviathan" is one of many terms associated with a particular view of demonic oppression. The basis of this belief comes from the characteristics of Leviathan's actions in the Bible and also from what we call deliverance ministries, which seek to exorcise those evil spirits. In some branches of the Charismatic movement, demons are considered the cause of almost every malady, hindrance, and problem.

Those who understand the leviathan spirit use references to the creature described in the book of Job and in verses such as Isaiah 27:1. The biblical descriptions are then given an entirely spiritual interpretation, rather than a physical one. Special emphasis is placed on the relationship of the Hebrew word *liw'yā'tān* to the concept of "twisting" or "coiling." Based on this, and little else, believers in the "leviathan spirit" extrapolate the existence of a specific demonic entity—"the leviathan spirit" or "the spirit of leviathan"—that oppresses people. The leviathan spirit is supposedly the cause of twisting the meaning of people's words, turning people against each other, and instigating unrest.

Others suggest that the "spirit of leviathan" causes stubbornness and rebellion against God. Alternatively, the spirit is blamed for various physical problems, mostly involving stiffness and back problems. Still others blame the leviathan spirit for insomnia, lack of spiritual growth, media deception, pride, reading disabilities, and/or personal bickering. Yet another group suggests that there are many "leviathan spirits," with or without some combination of those effects.

Scripture gives us every reason to believe there is a demonic entity named Leviathan or that Christians have the ability to rebuke or exorcise it. The Bible indicates that we are meant to diagnose spiritual problems by identifying a particular demon. Jesus did it on several occasions. A demonic entity may be involved in a person's spiritual struggle, but the Bible gives us clear guidelines for in "rebuking" it. Luke 10:19 declares that we have power to tread upon serpents and scorpions. Remedying the situation requires much prayer, fasting, and obedience to God.

IDENTIFYING THE LEVIATHAN SPIRIT

How do we go about overcoming a Leviathan spirit? First, we need to identify it.

In Job 41:34, it is called "king over all the children of pride," and pride is what allows this spirit to enter into people's lives. People who are guilty of pride and self-righteousness are affected by its influence.

The kind of pride we are talking about here is a prideful, puffed-up spirit, not to be confused with being proud of someone for doing something well, or being proud of a project you made, or an accomplishment.

Rather, when pride goes to a person's head and plants a seed in their heart, they begin the process of self-worship – that's being prideful, and that's the kind of pride I'm referring to.

Let's move on to the 12 characteristics of a Leviathan spirit that are commonly seen in its daily operation.

CHARACTERISTIC #1: THE LEVIATHAN SPIRIT TWISTS THE TRUTH

While it's true that all evil spirits are liars, the Leviathan spirit specializes in twisting the truth in the minds of its victims without them even realizing it. It twists intentions and conversations. Someone can tell them something, and they hear something totally different.

- Misinterpretation of what's said

- Anything positive is twisted

- Any type of correction is twisted, and the bringer becomes the enemy causing disunity.

- To get things to go their way, they manipulate.

- The person tells half-truths because, in their mind, they've told enough. Leviathan makes a person feel like if they tell the whole truth, their life will come to an end – invoking the spirit of fear to assist.

- Confusion

As you can imagine, this causes significant communications issues and division in relationships. These divisions cause hardness of heart, and in marriage, divorce. (Mathew 19:8) That is the goal of the Leviathan spirit; he's a covenant breaker.

CHARACTERISTIC #2: LEVIATHAN – TASKED WITH BREAKING COVENANTS

One of the primary missions of this demonic spirit is to destroy and break covenants. Leviathan hates covenants of any kind, especially the marriage covenant. It is responsible for nearly all, if not all, divorces.

A person working under the influence of Leviathan is so prideful that they can't admit when they're wrong. They play the blame game, and everything is always someone else's fault. This destroys relationships and creates division.

When there is division in a relationship, often both parties want it to end – they are in agreement with the division. Now, look at this scripture where Jesus is speaking:

"Again, truly I say to you that if two of you agree on earth about any matter that they ask, it will be done for them from my Father who is in heaven." (Matthew 18:19)

Although this is typically used for good, could the Leviathan spirit underhandly convince people to invoke it for evil purposes? The scripture doesn't specifically say "agree on earth about any good matter," it says any matter.

Demons twist God's word and spiritual laws to use them for evil purposes on a regular basis. How else could they gain an advantage in life?

God is not a liar. When he sets something in motion, it is set, period – for all. Demons look for loopholes and areas where they can twist what God has created.

Not only is it a characteristic of the Leviathan spirit to break covenants between humans, but it also rises against the covenant between God and man. This spirit doesn't want to work with anyone. And that leads us to the next characteristic.

CHARACTERISTIC #3: THE LEVIATHAN SPIRIT SEVERS YOUR RELATIONSHIP WITH GOD

The spirit of Leviathan is very effective at separating people from their relationship with God. It causes hardness of heart towards God too. It can do this by twisting scripture and whispering lies about God, stirring up feelings of anger, bitterness, unforgiveness, and resentment towards God. Thus says Yahweh: 'So I will ruin the pride of Judah and the great pride of Jerusalem. This evil people, who refuse to listen to my words, who go in the stubbornness of their hearts, and have gone after other gods, to serve them, and to bow in worship to them, let them be like this loincloth which is not good for anything.' Jeremiah 13:9-10 "Other gods" include Leviathan, pride, and self.

Once again, God was dealing with these spirits in Isaiah 6:9-10 when he said, Go and say to this people, 'Keep on listening and do not comprehend! And keep on looking and do not understand!'

Make the heart of this people insensitive, and make its ears unresponsive, and shut its eyes so that it may not look with its eyes and listen with its ears and comprehend with its mind and turn back, and it may be healed for him.'

Leviathan can also cause people to doubt God's goodness and love for them. They may believe that He is

45

uninvolved and distant in their lives as a result. They are left feeling lost, confused, and adrift.

CHARACTERISTIC #4: A LEVIATHAN SPIRIT IS STIFF-NECKED

Job 41:22-23 says, "Strength abides in its neck, and dismay dances before it. Its flesh's folds of skin cling together; it is cast on it—it will not be moved."

What does this look like in a person operating under the Leviathan spirit? They're very stubborn in believing that they know more than anyone else, and they are right. They don't want to do anything that isn't their idea first.

CHARACTERISTIC #5: THE LEVIATHAN SPIRIT IS HARD-HEARTED AND COLD

"Its heart is cast as stone; yes, it is cast as the lower millstone." Job 41:24

You'll notice that this spirit causes a person to become hard-hearted and coarse. They seem robot-like and have a nonchalant attitude of "whatever."

The definition of hard-hearted is incapable of being moved to pity or tenderness; unfeeling. They don't have empathy and have a hard time seeing things from another person's point of view.

The Leviathan spirit puts its scales up, engulfing the person under its influence so that even the truth bounces off them. In essence, the person is trapped inside, and their authentic self cannot get out.

CHARACTERISTIC #6: LEVIATHAN BLOCKS THE HOLY SPIRIT IN YOUR LIFE

In Job 41:15-17, the word air is the Hebrew word רה , 'Ruach' (Strong's 3707) translated as spirit. Talking about Leviathan...

"Its back has scales of shields; it is shut up closely as with a seal. They are close to one another— even the air cannot come between them. They are joined one to another; they cling together and cannot be separated."

The scales won't let the Holy Spirit in, blocking Him out. In fact, the scales block the expression of the real person trapped inside of them too.

CHARACTERISTIC #7: LEVIATHAN IS PROUD, HAUGHTY, AND ARROGANT

"It observes all the lofty (thinking they are better than others); he is a king over all the children of pride." Job 41:34

The spirit of Leviathan operates mainly through a prideful spirit. Often people become prideful because of a past rejection or trauma. The spirit of pride offers them the lie of power and a false sense of identity. It whispers, "You are really somebody," "You are special and not like anyone else." It causes the person to commit idolatry via self-worship.

But James 4:6 says that God resists the proud, so by agreeing with and operating in pride, the person cuts themselves off from God. What better way to keep someone in bondage than to offer them false power and separate them from God, the only one who can set them free?

Leviathan is a mocking spirit. Mockery is another way it attacks others. It will mock:

• People walking in the obedience of God.

    • Those who disagree with them (their own opinions are so important)

Mockery is defined as ridicule, contempt, making someone or something seem absurdly or offensively inadequate or unfitting. Part of mockery is dismissing something said as unimportant or stupid – invalidation.

CHARACTERISTIC #8: THE LEVIATHAN SPIRIT IS A WHISPERING LIAR

This spirit whispers lies (implants thoughts) which encourages false accusations against people, particularly those in positions of authority. It will plant outrageous seeds that are a complete distortion or twisting of the truth and then hammer those thoughts in over and over again.

Soon, the person is saying and doing what Leviathan wants because they don't know how to discern his lying thoughts from their own. Because of this, they latch on to the evil thoughts and claim them as their own – coming into agreement with the Leviathan spirit.

Out of the abundance of the heart, the mouth speaks. The "heart" is the mind, will, and emotions.

Luke 6:45: "The good person out of the good treasury of his heart brings forth good, and the evil person out of his evil treasury brings forth evil. For out of the abundance of the heart, his mouth speaks."

Matthew 12:34-37: "Offspring of vipers! How are you able to say good things when you are evil? For from the abundance of the heart, the mouth speaks.

The good person from his good treasury brings out good things, and the evil person from his evil treasury brings out evil things.

But I tell you that for every worthless word that they speak, people will give an account for it on the day of judgment! For by your words, you will be vindicated, and by your words, you will be condemned."

We should take every thought captive to the obedience of Christ to prevent an evil spirit's thoughts from taking root in our minds and then in our lives.

Pay attention to what you're thinking about! Is it a negative or dark feeling? Take it to the scriptures and compare them.

In 2 Corinthians 10:3-5, we are instructed:

"For although we are living in the flesh, we do not wage war according to the flesh, for the weapons of our warfare are not merely human, but powerful to God for the tearing down of fortresses (strongholds), tearing down arguments and all pride that is raised up against the knowledge of God, and taking every thought captive to the obedience of Christ."

I'd like to bring to your attention the word captive in that scripture. Captive is one forcibly taken in war.

This is a war in your mind, and you must put forth the effort to take those thoughts that don't line up with the Bible by force. Chop them down with the Sword of the Spirit by speaking what God says.

Just like Jesus did in the desert when Satan came against him with lies, twisting the scriptures, and testing his character. Matthew 3:4-11

CHARACTERISTIC #9: THE CONTENTIOUS LEVIATHAN SPIRIT

Leviathan uses contention and misunderstanding to destroy communication between people and God. This causes major division in relationships. If not stopped, this spirit will keep hammering the division with his manipulation and lies until the relationship is literally destroyed.

Strife is also one of his favorite methods of destruction. Strife is angry or bitter disagreement over fundamental issues or conflict.

Look at this scripture in Proverbs 2:20-28; it illustrates the contention of Leviathan clearly:

"For lack of wood, a fire goes out, and where there is no whisperer, quarreling will cease.

As charcoal is to hot embers and wood is to fire, so a man of quarrels is to kindling strife. The words of a whisperer are like delicious morsels, and they go down to the inner parts of the body. Like impure silver, which overlays an earthen vessel, so are smooth lips and an evil heart. On his lips, an enemy will pretend, but inside he will harbor deceit. When he makes his voice gracious, do not believe him, for seven abominations are in his heart.

Though hatred is covered with guile, its evil will be exposed in the assembly. He who digs a pit, in it he will fall, and he who rolls a stone, on him it will come back.

A tongue of deceit hates its victim, and a flattering mouth makes ruin."

In the book of Galatians, the Bible also warns us not to "bite or devour one another, lest you be consumed by one another.

A person who is operating under the guidance of Leviathan will speak destructive words that have a negative effect on the hearer. The words they speak pull down rather than build up.

They become more and more critical, especially of those in positions of power. A critical person can show criticism overtly through words and covertly through mannerisms.

CHARACTERISTIC #10: LEVIATHAN LIFTS UP LEADERS IN ORDER TO CRUSH THEM

Because Leviathan wants to do as much damage as possible to destroy covenant relationships, it tries to involve as many people as possible. What better way to do that than to target leaders and influencers?

The spirit of Leviathan will prey on pridefulness within that leader or influencer and use his worldly minions to raise the leader up in whatever position he holds. That could be multiple leadership positions in the same person.

For example, a husband who has been charged with leading his family and is also a leader in his job or the community. The higher Leviathan can bring him up, the further he can fall (with witnesses) when the principality decides to turn on him. This brings maximum destruction, affecting not only the leader but also everyone in covenant with him and even those who witness the fall.

"Pride comes before destruction and a haughty spirit before a fall. Better it is to be of a lowly (humble) spirit with the poor than to divide the spoil with the proud." Proverbs 16:18-19

CHARACTERISTIC #11: THE DEMONIC SPIRIT OF LEVIATHAN BRINGS DEPRESSION

Anytime you have a demonic presence operating in life, you will see depression accompany it at some point. This is the spirit of heaviness.

The human soul was not made to live in darkness and will wither in its continued presence.

Instead, one must turn to the light to be set free. Put on the garment of praise for the spirit of heaviness.

"The Spirit of the Lord God is upon me; Because the Lord hath anointed me to preach good tidings unto the meek; He hath sent me to bind up the brokenhearted, to proclaim liberty to the captives, And the opening of the prison to them that are bound; ...

To appoint unto them that mourn in Zion, to give unto them beauty for ashes, The oil of joy for mourning, The garment of praise for the spirit of heaviness; That they might be called trees of righteousness, The planting of the Lord, that he might be glorified." Isaiah 61:1-3

CHARACTERISTIC #12: LEVIATHAN, MASTER OF BLAME AND SELF-PITY

Because the leading way the Leviathan spirit operates is through pride, you'll see it rear its ugly horns when fault comes its way. It cannot be wrong or at fault for anything; it's too good for that – above it all.

So instead of humbling themselves, admitting when they're wrong, and making things right again, the person under the influence of pride and Leviathan will instead turn the blame on the other person. They will be able to feel major resistance rise up inside of them in these types of situations.

Some people's pride will pull in the spirit of anger to help out here by creating an anger wall (shield) so that no blame can enter.

CHARACTERISTICS OF THOSE OPERATING IN THE SPIRIT OF LEVIATHAN

One way you can tell if someone is operating under the control of a Leviathan spirit is to look at their attitude, way of thinking, and speech – their personality.

Demons have personalities; like people, they just don't have a physical body to accompany them. So, if you want to know what a demon's personality is like, look no further than the person it's possessing.

For a good tree bringeth not forth corrupt fruit; neither doth a corrupt tree brings forth good fruit. For every tree is known by its own fruit. For of thorns, men do not gather figs, nor of a bramble bush gather they grapes." Luke 6:43-44

CHAPTER 6

"THE LORD OF THE FLIES"

Beelzebub is the Greek form of the name *Baal-zebub*, a pagan Philistine god worshiped in the ancient Philistine city of Ekron during the Old Testament times. It is a term signifying "the lord of flies" (2 Kings 1:2). Archaeological excavations at ancient Philistine sites have uncovered golden images of flies. After the time of the Philistines, the Jews changed the name to "Beelzeboul," as used in the Greek New Testament, meaning "lord of dung." This name referenced the god of the fly that was worshiped to obtain deliverance from the injuries of that insect. Some biblical scholars believe Beelzebub was also known as the "god of filth," which later became a name of bitter scorn in the mouths of the Pharisees. As a result, Beelzebub was a particularly contemptible deity, and his name was used by the Jews as an epithet for Satan.

The word has two parts: *Baal,* which was the name for the Canaanite fertility gods in the Old Testament; and *Zebul,* which means "exalted dwelling." Putting the two parts together, they formed a name for Satan himself, the prince of demons. This term was first used by the Pharisees in describing Jesus in Matthew 10:24-25. Earlier, they had accused Jesus of casting "out the demons by the ruler of the demons" (Matthew 9:34), referencing Beelzebul (Mark 3:22; Matthew 12:24).

In Matthew 12:22 Jesus healed a demon-possessed man who was blind and mute. As a result, "all the people were astonished and said, 'Could this be the Son of David?' But when the Pharisees heard this, they denied that this could be a work of God, but instead declared: 'It is only by Beelzebub, the prince of demons, that this fellow drives out demons'" (Matthew 12:23-24).

It is remarkable that the Pharisees reacted to this incredible miracle by Jesus in the very opposite way of that of the multitude, who realized that Jesus was from God. In fact, it was an admission by the Pharisees that Jesus worked miracles or performed deeds beyond the reach of any unaided human power, but they attributed this power to Beelzebub instead of God. Actually, they should have known better: the devil cannot do works of pure goodness. However, in their self-absorbed pride, these Pharisees knew that, if the teachings of Jesus should prevail among the people, their influence over them was at an end. So, the miracle they did not deny, but instead attributed it to an infernal power, "Beelzebub the prince of the demons."

The greater question is this: what relevance does this have to us as Christians today? In Matthew 10, Jesus provides us with the very essence of what it means to be His disciple. Here we learn that He is about to send out His apostles into the world to preach the gospel (Matthew 10:7). He gives them specific instructions on what to do and what not to do. He warns them, "Be on your guard against men; they will hand you over to the local councils and flog you in their synagogues. All men will hate you because of me" (Matthew 10:17, 22). Then He adds, "A student is not above his teacher, nor a servant above his master. It is enough for the student to be like his teacher and the servant like his master. If the head of the house has been called Beelzebub, how much more the members of his household!" (Matthew 10:24-25).

The point Jesus is making to us today is that if people are calling Him Satan, as did the Pharisees of His time, they would surely call His disciples the same. In John chapter 15, Jesus declares, "If the world hates you, keep in mind that it hated me first. If you belonged to the world, it would love you as its own. As it is, you do not belong to the world, but I have chosen you out of the world. That is why the world hates you. Remember the words I spoke to you: 'No servant is greater than his master.' If they persecuted me, they will persecute you also. If they obeyed my teaching, they will obey yours also. They will treat you this way because of my name, for they do not know the One who sent me" (John 15:18-21).

In the time of Christ, this was the current name for the chief or prince of demons and was identified with SATAN (which see) and the DEVIL (which see). The Jews committed the unpardonable sin of ascribing Christ's work of casting out demons to Beelzebul, thus ascribing to the worst source the supreme manifestation of goodness (Matthew 10:25; 12:24, 27; Mark 3:22; Luke 11:15, 18, 19).

There can be little doubt that it is the same name as BAALZEBUB (which see). It is a well-known phenomenon in the history of religions that the gods of one nation become the devils of its neighbors and enemies. When the Aryans divided into Indians and Iranians, the Devas remained gods for the Indians, but became devils (daevas) for the Iranians, while the Ahuras remained gods for the Iranians and became devils (asuras) for the Indians. Why Baalzebub became Beelzebul, why the b changed into l, is a matter of conjecture. It may have been an accident of popular pronunciation, or a conscious perversion (Beelzebul in Syriac = "lord of dung"), or Old Testament zebhubh may have been a perversion, accidental or intentional of zebhul (= "house"), so that Baalzebul meant "lord of the house."

BEELZEBUB, THE PHARISEES, AND JESUS CHRIST

In **Matthew 12**, the Pharisees accuse Jesus of casting out demons by the power of "Beelzebub, the prince of demons." Read the full exchange here: *"Then a demon-oppressed man who was blind and mute was brought to him, and he healed him so that the man spoke and saw. And all the people were amazed, and said, "Can this be the Son of David?" But when the Pharisees heard it, they said, "It is only by Beelzebul, the prince of demons, that this man casts out demons." Knowing their thoughts, he said to them, "Every kingdom divided against itself is laid waste, and no city or house divided against itself will stand. And if Satan casts out Satan, he is divided against himself. How then will his kingdom stand? And if I cast out demons by Beelzebul, by whom do your sons cast them out? Therefore, they will be your judges. But if it is by the Spirit of God that I cast out demons, then the kingdom of God has come upon you."* (**Matthew 12:22-28**)

WHAT DOES BEELZEBUB DO?

In ancient religions, Beelzebub was associated with sacrifices. He was invoked to drive away the flies that always came as sacrifices were made and blood was shed. During the time of Jesus, Beelzebub became a prince of demons. The name became a reference to Satan and a distinct insult to Jesus.

Beelzebub was believed to be someone who could perform exorcisms. This deity had control of all the devilish behavior in the world. It could even possess people itself. Today, we lean toward the thought that Beelzebub is another name for Satan and has all the powers of Satan.

WHY DOES SATAN HAVE SO MANY NAMES?

Satan is one of many names for the evil Christians who fight every day. Other names include Prince of Darkness, Lucifer, Prince of Demons, Father of Lies, Moloch, and Antichrist. All these names refer to the same being. There is only one God with one name, yet Satan has many. Why?

Satan is considered the author of confusion. Having so many names solidifies that to be true. If Satan can use a different name in any given situation, humans are more likely to become confused and commit sin. Satan is cunning and uses his various names to play tricks on us and convince us that we are not doing the devil's bidding.

Satan's many names also describe his identity and actions. For example, the name devil means "false accuser" or "deceitful nature." Satan is a false accuser and deceives even those who love God. He is the tempter because he often leads us into temptation. He tempted Jesus in the wilderness. Satan is the serpent, and a snake can slither into places without us realizing it's there. It can hide itself well and make itself known in surprising ways.

Satan's many names are his weapons. He uses them against those who love the Lord and to keep those who don't know the Lord in the dark.

SHOULD WE AS CHRISTIANS BE WORRIED ABOUT SATAN?

Christians know that Christ has already won the war. Even so, we should still be concerned about the cunning, deceitful, and sly behaviors of Satan.

Satan can lead Christians into temptation. He can lead us to sin and cause us to stay in sin much longer than we want. He can cause division among Christians that ultimately leads to conflict in homes, churches, and families.

While Christians should be aware that Satan is real, we should not be consumed by the fear and worry of Satan. We should always remember what Scripture tells us about the God we serve. Our God has already provided the ultimate sacrifice for us. He has given us the Holy Spirit to guide our thoughts and actions. God has already given us the ending to the story in Revelation.

CHAPTER 7

"NIGHT TERROR SPIRITS"

THE MYTH, LEGEND, AND TALES ABOUT SUCCUBUS AND INCUBUS

The word incubus is derived from Late Latin root word incubate which means "lie on". We also get the Latin word incubo which means nightmare. These words describe the idea being communicated, of a demon (though to be male) that has sexual relations with women at night. Its female counterpart, succubus, is thought to be a female demon that has sex with men at night.

Numerous myths, legends, and tales have arisen regarding succubus and incubus or the experience. In fact, different regions in the world have different names for these demons. It turns out that the names "succubus and incubus" have been widely recognized. It is amazing how different unrelated cultures are trying to describe the same experience in different parts of the world. The key question is are these experiences real or are they legends and myths?

To help you better characterize the issue, let me suggest that you make a difference between the experience with this succubus and incubus demons and the stories that develop from them. These two are related but are not the same. The experience of a spiritual being engaging in sexual activities with people in their dreams is real. The stories, the explanations, possible solutions, and the whys may be many and form the basis of many developing myths and legends. Do not be deceived by the idea of legends and myths. Distinguish between the legends and myths and the experience.

This book is focused on explaining what the scriptures have to say about such demonic activities including that of succubus and incubus and especially to highlight the fact that these experiences are real and there is a spiritual solution. I have no interest getting into the details about the myths and legends, or a discourse on demonology.

SUCCUBUS AND INCUBUS IN THE SCRIPTURES

As believers, the Bible is the Word of God to guide our lives. The truth it contains should be the pillar upon which we judge every fact, knowledge, or experience. We should never be carried away by experiences only, especially when they stand against what the scriptures clearly teach us. I have heard some stories of people who had had experiences that are squarely non-biblical from the moment I heard them. Your only foundation against deception is your personal establishment of the truth. If God's Word abides in you, you will not be deceived. This is an essential warning before I engage with the experiences of demonic spirits.

Does the Bible have any direct references to succubus and incubus? No. Does the Bible call any of these "dream sex demons" by the names we use today? No. Does the Bible have anything to say about the activities of succubus and incubus or similar demonic spirits? Yes, and a lot is written. Someone will have to be literally blind if he or she reads the bible regularly and does not come across the realities of demonic spirits. Read the Gospels and watch how many times Jesus dealt with the activities of devils. I have met Christians who say they do not believe in demonic activity. What a tragedy! They say they do believe in God but do not believe in demons. How can that be? The God they believe in has warned us throughout the New Testament about the activities of Satan and his demons in our daily lives. Here are just two such verses.

For we do not wrestle against flesh and blood, but against the rulers, against the authorities, against the cosmic powers over this present darkness, against the spiritual forces of evil in the heavenly places. (Eph. 6:12 ESV)

Be sober-minded; be watchful. Your adversary the devil prowls around like a roaring lion, seeking someone to devour. (1 Pet. 5:8 ESV)

Lest Satan should get an advantage of us: for we are not ignorant of his devices. (2 Cor. 2:11 KJV)

The premise behind this sort of thinking is that many who live in the Western world think that demonic activity is restricted to witchcraft or similar things. God has never said that in the scriptures. Witchcraft is only a minority of the activity of demonic spirits. Satan and his demons operate in many subtle ways through simple everyday activities that many will never imagine could be spiritual. Please see the verses below

For though we walk in the flesh, we are not waging war according to the flesh. For the weapons of our warfare are not of the flesh but have divine power to destroy strongholds. We destroy arguments and every lofty opinion raised against the knowledge of God and take every thought captive to obey Christ, (2 Cor. 10:3-5 ESV)

Could you have imagined that demonic strongholds can manifest in the way people think? Well, if that is too much for you, take a look at the verse below.

And Peter took him aside and began to rebuke him, saying, "Far be it from you, Lord! This shall never happen to you." But he turned and said to Peter, "Get

behind me, Satan! You are a hindrance to me. For you are not setting your mind on the things of God, but on the things of man." (Matt. 16:22-23 ESV)

Did Jesus just call Peter Satan in the verse above? What did Peter do? Well, he simply voiced his concerns and suggested as a devoted follower that Jesus should not die on the cross. What in these verses suggested spiritual activity? Nothing—to you and me. However, with the discernment of the Spirit, Jesus saw who was speaking through Peter. Was Peter possessed by Satan? No. Did he lose his mind? No. Do you see what I mean? Satan and demons are more active than many believers realize. Sadly, many are either too superstitious because they lack discernment to know what is spiritual and what is natural while others are too modern with natural explanations for everything and have no clue when demonic activity is going on in their lives.

SUCCUBUS, INCUBUS AND CHRISTIANS

When it comes to spiritual warfare, I have encountered two dangerous extremes that we must avoid at all costs. The first group is those who seem to live for the purpose of fighting against demons. I call them the "super-spiritual." They are obsessed with demons, learn the names of all sorts of demons, see demons in everything that happens, and spend most of their time fighting with one demon or another. This is a dangerous place to be in. God has not called you to live to fight demons. You are called to live for God. Do not get distracted by demons. Christ, not demons, should be your focus. The truth about it is that if we focus on demons and pay attention to them long enough, we should not be surprised if they show up more in your lives, and we will indeed spend all of our time fighting with them.

At the other extreme are those Christians I will call "modern or civilized". They don't believe in "these things". I mentioned above how one believer told me that demons are restricted to developing countries. These sets of people have a natural explanation for everything that happens to them, including those who are spiritually triggered. They are spiritually blind, without discernment, and fail to recognize activities that are spiritual as opposed to purely natural. This mindset is as horrible as the first. Such Christians are those that are most liable to being oppressed for long periods by Satan because they are blinded to spiritual activities, exclusively seeking natural help for all their problems including those that are spiritual.

You should be in neither of these extremes. As a believer, the Lord wants you to keep your focus on Him, but not be ignorant of the spiritual activities of demons including succubus and incubus around you. Not everything that happens to you is demonic. However, disaster occurs when you are under a spiritual attack, and you have no idea of what is going on. Be vigilant. Be discerning. Listen and walk with the Holy Spirit.

INCUBUS AND SUCCUBUS TRUE STORIES

The experience of demonic spirits (the succubus and incubus) engaging with people in their dreams is real. There are two very important problems I have noticed by observation regarding this.

1. Many people have these experiences and are too ashamed and embarrassed about them. Don't suffer in silence from succubus or incubus. Open up and be free. Mind you, not every nightmare or wet dream is due to a demonic spirit. I have already discussed this above, and we must not be super-spiritual. However, be discerning to know when such experiences are spiritual. If they are, do not anguish in silence. Do something. Seek help.

2. Others who have these experiences think it is normal or maybe "others are having it too". Please do not console yourself with this deceptive thought. There is nothing normal about having sexual encounters with some demonic creature in your dreams.

MY EXPERIENCE

When I was a teenager, I began having some strange manifestations a while ago in which I would have a dream where I found myself having sex with a woman, sometimes I could not even identify who that person was. Was it just a dream? Absolutely not! What often woke me up from the dream was when I noticed that I was sensually sexually aroused and ejaculating. Every night this occurred to me, I initially thought that it was one of those things that happen to young people when they get too excited in their heads about sex. By then, as a young Christian, I knew I was not dealing with anything in the ordinary.

One of the things that happened to me that began ringing a spiritual bell in my head is was that every night I forgot to pray before going to bed, I was sure to have that dream. I remember moments when I used to get up at night after falling asleep without praying and became anxious about having this dream, and so I would run to my knees to pray.

I had no clue what I was doing that was causing this and how it came upon me. One thing I knew was that I was having a very strange experience that was clearly not normal. As I grew in faith, I actively sought deliverance from this personally and through ministers vested with the power of God operating in and through them. I got complete freedom. No more wet dreams. The truth is that anyone is free to explain that experience the way they choose to but when you get afflicted by things like these, your mindset is no longer about theories or what people think but about how to get free from the experience. My experience is on the lower end of what these demonic spirits do. People have experienced even worse manifestations.

THE SPIRITUAL EXPERIENCE WITH SUCCUBUS AND INCUBUS

I will divide the experience from succubus or incubus into two parts to aid our comprehension. The first part is the spiritual sexual encounter that occurs in dreams. The second part is the physical effects of that spiritual encounter. I have heard stories of people who may have serious marital crises with their spouses, such problems that you cannot put your finger on regarding what the big issue is. Others may experience financial crises or business failures once they have such sexual encounters. Yet others might lose potential marriage relationships. The physical effects can be multiple. The key is to avoid being super-spiritual or civilized as I mentioned above but discerning to know when these things are spiritual. Please do not go about saying your marital crises are all due to some succubus demon whereas it might not be. Discernment is personal and comes from the Spirit. If you are not prayerful, you will have a hard time with spiritual discernment, I hope this is not the case with you. The witness of the Spirit inside of you is your armor of discernment. I cannot explain to you how this works! The Spirit will lead and guide you into all truth and righteousness.

INCUBUS AND SUCCUBUS NAMES

Do not get carried away by the names of demons. The names "incubus" and "succubus" are only two of the many names that cultures across the world have called these demonic spirits. You can read Wikipedia to get a better understanding of the experiential and biblical realities we must deal with.

I think the most amazing descriptive names of succubus or incubus I have heard so far come from sub-Saharan Africa where these demons are called spiritual husbands and spiritual wives. No matter what the culture calls it, they are all describing the experience of demonic spirits having sexual encounters with people with tangible practical effects on their lives. I remember watching a documentary about Bobby Brown and he was telling a story about how he woke up in the middle of the night to a demonic spirit having sex with him.

DELIVERANCE FROM SUCCUBUS AND INCUBUS

Our Christian culture has come a long way in describing the activity of demons on people, from oppression, and depression to possession. Some are looking into whether there is a difference between demons, devils, and fallen angels. In fact, there are all sorts of questions if Christians can be possessed by demons or not. When you are tormented by an evil spirit such as incubus or succubus, you certainly will care less whether is possession or oppression or whatever it is. You want the activity to stop. And that is what God wants also. That process by which the activity of an evil spirit operating in someone's life is terminated is essentially what deliverance is. It means stopping that activity and/or driving the spirit away (casting out) and freeing that individual from the control of those spirits. Jesus' earthly ministry was replete with casting demons out.

ACCESSING POWER AND AUTHORITY

You can break the power of succubus and incubus over your life. However, if you cannot muster the spiritual stamina needed, seek help. God has ordained and anointed ministers to help his children. Seeking help or seeking a miracle from another believer who is endowed with a gift you do not have is not wrong. In fact, it rather acknowledges the fact that God deals with us as a family. I have met people who are suffering from some oppression and "they have been praying and fasting about it" for 2, 5, or even 10 years. You do not need to suffer this long when God has ordained ministers around you who can help you. Seek help in the Body of

Christ when you need it. Don't suffer in your little corner with an embarrassing situation just because you are trying to make it happen on your own. I will encourage you to start with your Pastor right where you are. If help is not found there, do not stop seeking but continue.

CHAPTER 8

SPIRIT OF JEZEBEL

Jezebel is mentioned in the Bible over 22 times, mostly in 1 Kings 18, but also again in Revelation 2. In other portions of Scripture, fear and heaviness are called spirits, but the Bible does not directly call Jezebel a spirit. For God has not given us a *spirit of fear*, but of power and of love and of a sound mind. To console those who mourn in Zion, to give them beauty for ashes, The oil of joy for mourning, The garment of praise for the *spirit of heaviness;* That they may be called trees of righteousness, The planting of the Lord, that He may be glorified." Is

So why do Christians call Jezebel a spirit?

It is because of her reappearance in the book of Revelation that the idea of a spirit was derived.

Nevertheless, I have a few things against you, because you allow that woman Jezebel, who calls herself a prophetess, to teach and seduce My servants to commit sexual immorality and eat things sacrificed to idols. Rev 2:20

Due to this verse, we can assume that Jezebel is a demonic spirit that inhabits a person and causes them to be control-driven, a promoter of false teaching, and heavily driven by sexual appetite.

The best way to define this spirit is by looking at the example Jezebel herself lived (1 Kings 18). She lived a life of immorality, idolatry, false teachings, and unrepented sins. She was not guided by principles or restrained by a fear of God or man. She was passionate in her pursuit and heavily attached to heathenistic worship.

JEZEBEL IN THE NEW TESTAMENT

And I gave her time to repent of her sexual immorality, and she did not repent. Indeed, I will cast her into a sickbed, and those who commit adultery with her into great tribulation, unless they repent of their deeds. I will kill her children with death, and all the churches shall know that I am He who searches the minds and hearts. And I will give to each one of you according to your works. Rev 2:21-23

If you read the context of this chapter, you will notice that it was the church that had Jezebel operating in high levels of the church. As surprising as that may seem, it is not at all uncommon to see. So here are a few characteristics and truths to note and be aware of so you can steer clear of this spirit.

8 CHARACTERISTICS OF THE SPIRIT OF JEZEBEL

1. It Operates in Men and Women

I remember a time when I was doing deliverance on this man and the spirit of Jezebel manifested. It had been causing lust in his life and after the guy was delivered, he was free from pornography. It is a lie that this spirit only operates in women through the means of control.

2. It Causes Control, Manipulation, & Domination (A Form of Witchcraft)

Manipulation, intimidation, and the desire or impulse to control people is a characteristic of Jezebel.

The Bible says the fruit of the Holy Spirit is,

"But the fruit of the Spirit is love, joy, peace, forbearance, kindness, goodness, faithfulness, gentleness, and *self-control*..." Gal 5:22

The fruit of Jezebel is people's control. It causes a desire to control the surroundings and even people, while never producing "self-control."

3. It Causes Fear, Flight, and Discouragement

Jezebel is good at causing intimidation in people.

Scripture highlights that she didn't *kill* Elijah, she simply sent a messenger to discourage him and make him run in fear of his life.

Elijah was afraid when he got her message, and he ran to the town of Beersheba in Judah. He left his servant there, then walked another whole day into the desert. Finally, he came to a large bush and sat down in its shade. He begged the Lord, "I've had enough. Just let me die! I'm no better off than my ancestors." 1Kings 19:3-4

Elijah was a powerful man of God. He brought fire down from heaven with his command; he seemed fearless! However, this threat was enough to instill fear and even depression in his life. This happened shortly after he had such a great victory on Mount Carmel (1 Kings 18).

A lot of times, after great victories, this spirit will try and bring deep despair to a person. They might even feel as though they don't want to live, and it causes cycles of burnout.

If the enemy can't attack you head-on, he will wear you out.

Learn to find comfort in the still, quiet voice of the Holy Spirit.

4. It Seduces and Provokes Sexual Immorality

Revelation says, you allow Jezebel, who calls herself a prophetess, to teach and seduce My servants to commit sexual immorality...Rev 2:20

Many of us have heard stories of men of God who have fallen into this sin. They have been seduced, have come under discouragement, and have fallen into the enemy's trap.

When Jehu came to destroy Jezebel, she came out of the window and made sure to have makeup on. Her plan was to seduce Jehu.

Jezebel is after ministers of God. This is very common because of the authority in which they stand. When someone in authority falls, the news doesn't just affect the immediate family, but it also affects those who believe in them and follow their ministry.

Take time to pray for your pastors, for the men and women God has placed in leadership roles around you. The higher that God takes a person, the more the enemy wants to attack them and so they will fall into sin, affecting the faith of many as a result.

When David committed sexual immorality with Bathsheba, the Lord said,

However, because by this deed you have given great occasion to the enemies of the LORD to blaspheme…" 2 Sam 12:14

His sin had given leeway for others to doubt and blaspheme the God that David served. The enemy will often use this tactic to cause ministers of God to fall into pornography, adultery, and other sexual sins.

5. Loves Leadership Positions

Jezebel was not just a servant; she was a queen. In Revelation, we see that she was a prophetess. I am always cautious when I see young men or women who seem to love the spotlight. They can't live without a microphone or a podium because it feeds a sense of worth and value.

It is dangerous to feed this insecurity through this means. By doing so, you can unknowingly allow this spirit to overtake you, and begin to influence the church and the kingdom of God through your desire for fame. Then, instead of being used by God, you will be a puppet for the enemy's schemes.

6. Thrives Where Leadership is Weak

For every Jezebel, there is an Ahab.

Ahab has a very passive character and was unwilling to confront Jezebel. God had to send Jehu to take her out because Ahab couldn't.

Jezebel thrives in areas where leadership is afraid of confrontation.

When leadership is passive and fears any conflict that may occur when confronting Jezebel, they are acting just as Ahab did—enabling.

We don't have to love confrontation, but part of the challenge of being in leadership in the church or being a pastor is spotting and confronting Jezebel. To do that you must have the spirit of Elijah, the characteristic that he displayed when he fought the evil brought about by her.

Before you run off and confront everyone that you don't get along with within the church, deal with Jezebel within your own life. Certain habits, desires for control, discouragements, sexual sins, desires for fame—deal with these areas first before you deal with them in others. Afterward, don't be afraid of men, but confront those behaviors.

7. Not Repentant

Jezebel is usually not repentant. We see in 1 King that she never repented, she had to be punished. And in the book of Revelation, God gives her a chance to repent, but she is unwilling.

I have given her time to repent of her immorality, but she is unwilling. Rev2:21

There are consequences to allowing this wicked spirit to operate in your life. If you notice your behavior being influenced by this spirit or others around you, repent and confront that witch head-on.

Don't give a place to Jezebel in your life.

You can overcome Jezebel by the blood of Jesus, repentance of sin, and seeking to bear the fruit of the Holy Spirit.

CHAPTER 9

THE SPIRIT OF LILITH

The spirit of Lilith is very sneaky and can often be confused with Jezebel, as she shares some of the characteristics of the Jezebel spirit. Lilith can come in through receiving an abortion, generational curses, soul ties, or other sexual sins. She can enter through other sins but is most prevalent when coming through open doors in the above areas. Lilith is ruthless and will not leave without deliverance or the hand of God.

Lilith is known as the mother of demons. She is related to the succubus spirit. She can and will behave like a succubus, however, she goes much further than a succubus ever will. She prefers to be attached to women however, men are an easy target to get to the next woman and will attack men readily to lead them astray in sexual sin. Satanists refer to her as the wife of Samael, which is a fallen angel and not Satan. This is how she is known as the mother of demons. Biblically she is also noted as the screech owl. It is also what denotes where much of the retaliation and retribution comes from when dealing with this demon, as she has much-fallen angel backing. Demons do reproduce other demons as one manner of where they come from. Lilith however is not and was not Adam's first wife. Scripture does not lie or cover things up.

She has many characteristics that you may notice manifesting in a person she is attached to or in. Firstly, let's look at some of the less-known qualities. Lilith is also a type of vampire spirit. We will get into what that causes in just a moment. Just as there are many demons known as kings and princes of hell, Lilith is one of the queens of hell. She is quite conceited due to this fact. She herself hates human children. She is very lustful and haughty. She is disobedient and disrespectful of male authority. Lilith is also a witch, so she throws word curses, curses operate in New Age, black magic, and also in divination and necromancy. This spirit also leaves behind barren land, famine in different areas of life, and other signs.

Let's look at some of the signs of demonization concerning the spirit of Lilith. Lilith causes abortions, so someone who is pro-choice may be showing signs of Lilith. However, this alone is not nearly enough to determine that Lilith is present, as this is indicative of the enemy in general. Miscarriages are another sign of the presence of Lilith. She cannot stand human children or mankind at all so she seeks to prevent human reproduction as much as possible. With this battle, a woman may notice heavy, irregular or problematic monthly cycles. A person who is demonized or oppressed by her may notice an irregular presence of owls. Frequent illness in children can also be a sign of Lilith. Since Lilith is a vampire spirit, you may notice fatigue and exhaustion in this person. They may always seem drained. They may also constantly want attention in some way and be jealous of others regularly. Chaos will be present in their life instead of order, and they will cause chaos and confusion often as well. There may be marital problems due to the lack of biblical order in the house similar to what Jezebel causes. Women may be unwilling to submit to their husbands or other roles of male authority. A person may exhibit uncontrollable behavior. Strong delusional feminism is another sign of Lilith's presence. You may also see bisexual tendencies, attractions, or curiosities. Lilith is commonly thought to be responsible for things such as SIDS and other infirmities that attack children under a year old. Please note that all these things do not need to be present for Lilith to be there; however, you also cannot assume that you are dealing with Lilith based on one or two of these items either.

As always follow the guidance of the Holy Spirit to discern what spirits you are dealing with or in bondage to. These lists of characteristics and signs of demonization are by no means exhaustive and there are many more. We hope this book has helped you recognize and know your enemy enough to fight it and cast it out.

CHAPTER 10

THE PLACE OF POWER AND AUTHORITY

One of the dilemmas of the modern church in most places today is that some might recognize demons but are powerless to command their activities to stop or cast them out. It is one thing to identify a demon. It is another to be able to cast it out. Demons do not answer to theology or doctrine. They answer to power and authority. Though every believer has the Holy Spirit living inside of them and therefore has power within them, not every believer is able to unleash or manifest that power. In fact, not every minister is also able to manifest that power. This is not only embarrassing to us as Christians, but it is also for the world that comes to the Church for help in spiritual matters only to meet believers who are also helpless themselves.

Jesus said, and *these signs shall follow them that believe; In my name shall they cast out devils; they shall speak with new tongues; (Mk. 16:17 KJV)*

That means every believer has the inherent power to cast out demons. The problem then is not because they are not believers but that many believers are just not spiritually mature or equipped. I met someone who asked me if they had to visit some "deliverance minister" to get delivered and why they could not do it themselves. The truth is that you do not have to visit a minister to get delivered. Jesus said as a believer, you can speak to demons. The problem is that many believers cannot speak with authority. Many believers do not know the Word, and many more do not have a consistent prayer life or feed on the scriptures. We cannot ignore our spiritual lives all day and all week and think we will speak to a demon, and it will hear us. It does not work that way. If you build up your spirit with the Word and yield to the Spirit, you can speak to any spirit and deliver yourself. I remember also praying and even fasting on my own and that dirty spirit just kept tormenting me. Don't suffer alone. If you cannot get it done yourself, seek help from ministers who clearly have God's power operating in them.

EXERCISING AUTHORITY

Demons, such as succubus or incubus, respond to spiritual authority. By default, every believer has been lifted up far above all demonic powers.

Far above all principality, and power, and might, and dominion, and every name that is named, not only in this world but also in that which is to come (Eph. 1:21 KJV)

The Holy Spirit that lives in the believer is the Finger of God that subdues all demonic powers.

But if I with the finger of God cast out devils, no doubt the kingdom of God is come upon you. (Lk. 11:20 KJV)

But if I cast out devils by the Spirit of God, then the kingdom of God is come unto you. (Matt. 12:28 KJV)

Authority is exercised through words. Words of authority are used to cast out succubus or incubus demons. As I mentioned above, there are believers who speak to demons and get a response while others speak to demons, and nothing happens. The difference is the degree of authority working in their words. The rod of exercising authority over demonic spirits is words of power.

When the even has come, they brought unto him many that were possessed with devils: and he cast out the spirits with his word, and healed all that were sick: (Matt. 8:16 KJV)

How do you do this? There are no rituals needed. All you need to do is to open your mouth and command succubus or incubus and it will obey you. Yes, it is that simple if power is in your mouth. You can do this right from your home, right now. Declare that "In the Name of Jesus I command every spiritual influence to leave my life right now".

STEPS TO BE FREE FROM THESE DEMONS

How Satan Operates

1. Influence: subtle influence of our attitudes, behaviors,

2. Oppression: Demonic power having access to inflict pain, without living in you.

3. Possession: A spirit being living in a person

Discernment is key: Not everything in our lives that is wrong is related to a demon.

Deliverance

Breaking free from the influence, oppression, or possession of devils.

Power is what is needed to influence.

Only one place you will find this power: His Name is Jesus.

You will not find the power to chase demons in the world.

How To Be Delivered

1. Be Saved from Sin and Satan's Grip

The sinner is in Satan's camp and territory.

To open their eyes and turn them from darkness to light, and from the power of Satan to God, so that they may receive forgiveness of sins and a place among those who are sanctified by faith in me.' (Acts 26:18 NIV)

Being baptized according to Acts 2:38 for the remission of sin is a critical part of the salvation process. As well as being filled with the Holy Spirit Acts 2:16. You can't have one without the other. They go together like a hand in a glove.

Receiving Christ is crucial for your freedom from demonic activity. It is the beginning.

The sinner lives separated from God; a state called spiritual death. Satan is the lord of death right now.

Since the children have flesh and blood, he too shared in their humanity so that by his death he might break the power of him who holds the power of death— that is, the devil — (Heb. 2:14 NIV)

Satan rules in death. Outside of God, he is the king.

Trying to attack Satan without being saved will lead to a spiritual catastrophe as seen below.

Some Jews who went around driving out evil spirits tried to invoke the name of the Lord Jesus over those who were demon-possessed. They would say, "In the name of the Jesus whom Paul preaches, I command you to come out." Seven sons of Sceva, a Jewish chief priest, were doing this. One day the evil spirit answered them, "Jesus I know, and Paul I know about, but who are you?" Then the man who had the evil spirit jumped on them and overpowered them all. He gave them such a beating that they ran out of the house naked and bleeding. (Acts 19:13-16 NIV)

2. Close the Open Doors

And do not give the devil a foothold (Eph. 4:27 NIV).

Satan has footholds that give him access and the right to exercise his power and influence.

Important footholds for our discussion.

• Sin, especially sexual sin, pornography, etc.

• Occultic practices

• Emotional footholds such as bitterness.

What should you do now?

- Confess any sin to the Lord, repent, and ask for forgiveness

- Renounce every demonic involvement you have been involved in

3. Command Satan and Evil Spirits To Leave!

Words are the most important vessel for communicating God's power.

Very important statement.

Spirits respond to words of authority.

When evening came, many who were demon-possessed were brought to him, and he drove out the spirits with a word and healed all the sick (Matt. 8:16 NIV)

They do not respond to spiritual drama, noise, crying, incantations, counseling, etc

Through Counseling is helpful and has its place to solve problems such as behavior or attitude issues, it has no value in demonic matters. If a demon is involved, the only way forward is getting that demon out or break its power.

This is the reason I mentioned above that discernment is important: demons are not always responsible, but we should know when they are involved.

Words are the rod that controls demons.

How do you drive out demons?

You command them to leave in Jesus Name!

Example of Paul

Once when we were going to the place of prayer, we were met by a female slave who had a spirit by which she predicted the future. She earned a great deal of

money for her owners by fortune-telling. She followed Paul and the rest of us, shouting, "These men are servants of the Most High God, who are telling you the way to be saved." She kept this up for many days. Finally, Paul became so annoyed that he turned around and said to the spirit, "In the name of Jesus Christ I command you to come out of her!" At that moment the spirit left her. (Acts 16:16-18 NIV)

The only people who can do this are Christians because they are saved.

Your turn

Please say these words with me:

"In the name of Jesus, I command every evil spirit to leave my life right now. I command every satanic oppression and influence over my life to stop."

It is that simple. These are spiritual things, and they work by spiritual principles and not by what makes sense to our minds

Power can also be transmitted through laying of hands and objects such as handkerchiefs, aprons, or anointing oil and water.

God did extraordinary miracles through Paul, so that even handkerchiefs and aprons that had touched him were taken to the sick, and their illnesses were cured, and the evil spirits left them. (Acts 19:11-12 NIV)

Every believer can do this, but many are not spiritually established.

They do not believe, they do not pray, etc.

You do not need to be a pastor, command the devil to leave your life right now.

4. Seek Another Believer Or Man or Woman of God To Pray And Deliver You.

Though speaking about casting out demons is simple, it takes faith and spiritual maturity to do it. Sadly, not every believer is prepared spiritually to do this. Furthermore, if you are not a Christian, you cannot attempt to do this, or you might get in trouble since God's power and protection are not on you. I recommend you seek another Christian or minister who can deliver you. As noted above, if your pastor does not believe in this or is not able to help you, seek help from another minister.

ABOUT THE AUTHOR

Billy E. Chatman Jr was born On June 23, 1972, In Tampa Florida. His parents were in the Air Force, so they traveled around the world in his childhood. In the midst of the traveling, his father was stationed at Dyess A.F.B, Abilene, TX. It was there that he met his high school sweetheart, Nicci Chatman. They both graduated from Cooper High School and have been married for 31 years. They also have two children Billy 3rd and Reonna Chatman.

Pastor Chatman joined the Louisville Fire & Rescue at the age of 19 years old. After advancing to the position of Captain he was forced to Retire due to being diagnosed with Multiple Sclerosis. After his retirement, he founded a church called Temple of Deliverance Worship Center. In 2008 he was appointed as the Tri-State youth president of Kentucky, Ohio, & West Virginia. Where he held youth conferences.

In 2011 God spoke to Pastor Chatman to move to his hometown of Tampa, Florida, and start a church there. In 2018 he had the opportunity to join the Tampa Police Department where he currently serves on the Reserve Unit. Pastor Chatman also founded his own nonprofit organization, Natural Bourne Leaders Academy. This is a program designed for at-risk teens, that will develop the leader within them. My passion is to help develop the next generation of leaders. Our motto is "SHAPING TODAY YOUTH N2 TOMORROW's LEADERS".

Thank you for reading my book. Please leave a review on Amazon or Barnes & Noble.

CONCLUSION

In conclusion, the topic of deliverance from demonic spirits is a complex and often controversial one. However, through the exploration of various personal testimonies and scriptural references, it becomes clear that the reality of demonic oppression is a very real and pressing concern for many people. Whether through prayer, spiritual counseling, or other means, those who have experienced deliverance from demonic spirits often report a sense of profound relief and renewed spiritual strength. It is important to remember that everyone's experience with deliverance will be different and being under a Pastor that believes in the fivefold gifts of the ministry is always important. Beware of these ancient spirits that want to have a love affair with your soul. These spirits are playing for keeps because they know that their time is limited on this earth. Ultimately, the power of God and the transforming nature of faith can provide hope, healing, and deliverance for those struggling with demonic possession.